Profiles in American History

The Life and Times of

SUSAN B. ANTHONY

Mitchell Lane
PUBLISHERS

P.O. Box 196 · Hockessin, Delaware 19707

Titles in the Series

The Life and Times of

SUSAN B. ANTHONY

Tamra Orr

Mitchell Lane
PUBLISHERS

Copyright © 2007 by Mitchell Lane Publishers, Inc. All rights reserved. No part of this book may be reproduced without written permission from the publisher. Printed and bound in the United States of America.

Printing   1   2   3   4   5   6   7   8   9

Library of Congress Cataloging-in-Publication Data
Orr, Tamra.
    The life and times of Susan B. Anthony / by Tamra Orr.
        p. cm. — (Profiles in American history)
    Includes bibliographical references and index.
    ISBN 1-58415-445-4 (lib. bdg. : alk. paper)
    1. Anthony, Susan B. (Susan Brownell), 1820–1906—Juvenile literature. 2. Feminists—United States—Biography—Juvenile literature. 3. Suffragists—United States—Biography—Juvenile literature. 4. Women's rights—United States—History—Juvenile literature. I. Title. II. Series.
HQ1413.A55O77   2006
305.42092—dc22   2005036699

ISBN-10: 1-58415-445-4   ISBN-13: 9781584154457

ABOUT THE AUTHOR: Tamra Orr is a full-time author and writer living in the Pacific Northwest. She has written more than 50 nonfiction books for kids and adults and hopes to reach 100 in her lifetime. She is the author of *The Dawn of Aviation and the Story of the Wright Brothers* for Mitchell Lane Publishers, as well as several books about soccer in Mitchell Lane's No Hands Allowed series. She is mother to four and says that between them and her research, she learns something new every single day.

PHOTO CREDITS: Cover—North Wind Picture Archives; pp. 1, 3, 6, 9, 10, 12, 17, 18, 20, 24, 26, 28, 31, 33, 34, 36, 40, 41—Library of Congress.

PUBLISHER'S NOTE: This story is based on the author's extensive research, which she believes to be accurate. Documentation of such research is contained on page 46.
    The internet sites referenced herein were active as of the publication date. Due to the fleeting nature of some web sites, we cannot guarantee they will all be active when you are reading this book.

PLB

Profiles in American History

Contents

*For Your Information

Anthony stands in front of her Madison Street home where she was arrested in 1872. Her crime was voting in a local election.

CHAPTER
1

A Knock on the Door

On a sunny autumn day in 1872, a United States deputy marshal, dressed properly in a beaver hat and gloves, slowly got out of his horse-drawn carriage. He walked up to the front door of Susan B. Anthony's home on Madison Street and knocked. In his hand, he held important papers that would immediately cause a stir in his city of Rochester, New York. It would also be the first step in an event that would go down in almost every history book.

E. J. Keeney's visit was no surprise. In fact, Anthony had been waiting for almost two weeks for him to come by. Thirteen days earlier, she and her three sisters, Guelma, Hannah, and Mary, had voted in the town's local election. She knew she would be arrested for doing so. The entire country knew that women were not allowed to vote in any kind of election.

Keeney was led to the parlor, where he met with the bold and confident Anthony. "He sat down," said Anthony later. "He said it was pleasant weather. He hemmed and hawed and finally said Mr. Storrs wanted to see me. 'What for?' I asked. 'To arrest you,' said he. 'Is that the way you arrest men?' 'No.' Then I demanded that I should be arrested properly." According to many different stories, Anthony insisted that she be allowed to change clothes and then be handcuffed like any other criminal. "My sister desiring to go

with me he proposed that he should go ahead and I follow with her," Anthony added. "This I refused and he had to go with me. In the horse-drawn car he took out his pocketbook to pay fare. I asked if he did that in his official capacity. He said yes; he was obliged to pay the fare of any criminal he arrested. Well, that was the first cents worth I ever had from Uncle Sam."[1]

Anthony's moment in court was still several months away. Already, her face and her message were known by hundreds of people. For years, she had dedicated her life to fighting for equal rights for her gender. The Civil War had taught the country that African American men should be treated the same as white men. They had become legal citizens who could own property, get an education, and vote. Women, however, white or black, did not have the same rights. They could not inherit family property, pursue schooling, or get a divorce. They were paid far less to do a job than men were for the same work. Other careers were forbidden to them completely. The only jobs they could typically hold at that time were teacher, nurse, farm help, factory worker, mill girl, or maid.

Unlike what it may seem, this treatment of women was not because they were seen as stupid or unimportant, although some people did feel that way. Many people believed that women were the better sex. They were thought to be gentle, pure, and moral creatures. They were in charge of taking care of the hearth, meaning the home and children. Getting involved in issues like politics would be dangerous for them, some believed. Women would lose their special innocence. They would be exposed to events that included activities like smoking cigarettes, guzzling beer, and telling sexual jokes. It would change the balance in the household and what jobs and duties men and women were expected to do. Cartoons and drawings were printed in newspapers and magazines, showing men holding babies and washing dishes while their cigar-smoking, pants-wearing wives headed out the door to vote. The image was frightening to many families. They thought family life would completely fall apart.

Many women accepted life and their role in it just as it was. They did not really want things to change. They liked staying out

of "men's topics" like politics, business, and war. They had plenty of other concerns to keep them busy. Other women, including Susan B. Anthony, Amelia Bloomer, Lucretia Mott, and Elizabeth Cady Stanton, fought against what they felt was a great injustice against their sex. They wanted to have a voice and play a part in the world and what happened in it. Being a woman was no reason, they firmly believed, to be left out of this. They could have their opinions and still remain honorable wives and mothers. Their presence in areas that currently belonged only to men would improve them, they believed. It would make them more honest.

The issue of women's rights was a growing one. There were determined people on both sides of the argument. For the first

Lucretia Mott (1793–1880), together with other reformers, organized the first woman's rights convention in New York. As well as working for women's rights, Mott was one of the first female Quaker leaders to work to abolish slavery.

Elizabeth Cady Stanton, mother of seven, was a staunch women's rights advocate. She was also a lifelong friend to Anthony. The daughter she holds, Harriot, would also be a leader in the women's rights movement.

time, a number of women were actively getting involved with national issues like slavery and temperance. They were not staying back and keeping quiet any longer. Instead, they were out there getting signatures on petitions, giving speeches, making signs, and writing papers.

Of all those women, few were as passionate, determined, and just plain noisy as Susan B. Anthony. She was sometimes called the Napoleon of the Women's Suffrage Movement. Her words and her actions would come to stand for a battle that would take a century to win: women's right to vote.

In Statue and Coin

To honor the work of Susan B. Anthony, as well as Elizabeth Cady Stanton and Lucretia Mott, a monument was sculpted by Adelaide Johnson from an eight-ton block of Italian marble. It was unveiled in the Capitol Rotunda in 1921 on what would have been Anthony's 101st birthday. For many years, it was kept in a quiet little corner of the Capitol. In 1997, it was relocated to the Rotunda. The inscription on the monument reads, in part:

> The three great destiny characters of the world whose spiritual import and historical significance transcend that of all others of any country or age.
>
> Lucretia Mott and Elizabeth Cady Stanton in the call of that first woman's rights convention of 1848 *initiated* and Susan B. Anthony *marshalling* the latent forces through three generations *guided* . . . the only fundamental universal uprising on our planet. *The woman's revolution.*
>
> Principle not policy; justice, not favor; men, their rights and nothing more; women, their rights and nothing less, was the clarion call to the most astounding upheaval of all time. A call which waked the world, signaled and inaugurated a revolution without tradition or precedent, and proclaimed the first incontrovertible concept of human freedom—that of individual liberty—personal responsibility, including women.
>
> Woman, first denied a soul, then called mindless, now arisen declared herself an entity to be reckoned. . . .
>
> Historically these three stand unique and peerless.[2]

In addition, in 1979, a new dollar coin (left) was issued from the U.S. Mint with the image of Anthony on it. She was the first woman to be shown on U.S. money. However, the shape of the coin was so close to that of the quarter that it was not popular. In 1999, the coin was replaced with a larger golden one bearing the image of Shoshone interpreter and guide Sacagawea.

Despite her stern appearance, Anthony was a happy woman with a sense of humor. She was well liked by many.

CHAPTER
2

Growing Up, Taking Stands

Looking at old black-and-white photos of Susan Brownell Anthony, it is hard to imagine that she was actually a fun-loving, happy, and kind person. The fashion of the day and her choice of stark clothing and hairstyle often made her look stern, angry, and rather unlikable. Nothing could be further from the truth. She was a friendly and charming person. She also showed her ability to dig in her heels and stick up for what she believed in from an early age.

Anthony was born February 15, 1820, in Adams, Massachusetts. She was second of six children. (The Anthonys had eight children, but two died in infancy.) Her mother, Lucy Read, was a Baptist who had done the unthinkable: She married a Quaker. Daniel Anthony's religious beliefs changed her life. No longer could she wear bright colors, dance, or even listen to music. Despite these restrictions, her husband was a kind man. Daniel, who ran a cotton mill, took good care of his employees, giving them clothing, food, a place to live, and education for their children.

Susan was a very bright child. By the time she was three years old, she could already read and write. As Quakers, she and her brothers and sisters were not allowed to play with toys or games. Instead they spent their time making up stories, reading, playing in the snow, and visiting their grandparents.

In elementary school, she came up against her first conflict over being female. She enjoyed math and wanted to learn how to do long division. Her teacher did not agree. "A girl needs to know how to read her Bible and count her egg money, nothing more," she was told.[1] When her father found out what had happened, he was angry and disappointed in the school. He felt that all people, regardless of their gender, had the right to a full education and the skills to earn a living. He took his children out of school and set up a home school for them. His employees' children attended as well. Their teacher, Mary Perkins, inspired Susan. First, she taught the boys and girls as equals. Second, she showed the girls that women could work and earn a wage.

When Susan was eleven, she spent some time helping her father in his mill. While there, she saw a female worker who clearly knew the job better than her boss. She told her father to promote the woman to overseer. Daniel refused. He said, "It would never do to have a woman overseer in the mill."[2] It was an attitude he would change later in life.

As a teenager, Susan and her sister Guelma were sent to Deborah Moulson's Female Seminary, one of the country's rare female boarding schools. There she took classes in everything from algebra and philosophy to literature and bookkeeping. Although the school was considered a good one, Susan was terribly homesick. Moulson, the headmistress, was strict and unkind. As hard as Susan tried to do well, she was frequently punished. Once she was in trouble simply because she forgot to dot a few of the i's in her essay! She began to lose confidence in her ability as a student. In her diary, she wrote, "Perhaps the reason I cannot see my own defects is because my heart is hardened."[3] It was not long before she began to think of herself as "the worst girl of all being."[4]

Susan's rescue from her life at Moulson's finally came, but it was a sad one. In 1837, the economy dropped. People everywhere were out of jobs and money, including the Anthony family. They were on the edge of bankruptcy. Since the money to pay for their school was gone, Susan and Guelma had to return home. Susan was not sad to say goodbye. She was happy to go back to her family. Wanting to help them in whatever way she could, she'd spend

her days spinning wool, quilting, building furniture, cooking, and baking. She also took a job in New Rochelle as a teacher at a Quaker girls' school to help bring in money.

Despite everyone's hard work, the family lost everything. To pay their creditors, they had to give up their house and all its contents—from furniture and silverware to clothing and food. Even wedding presents and the family Bible were seized. According to biographer Ida Husted Harper, "The underclothes of wife and daughters; spectacles of Mr. and Mrs. Anthony, pocketknives of the boys and even scraps of old iron" were removed.[5] The family had no choice but to move. They went to Hardscrabble, New York. It was not long before Susan was bored with her work at the girls' school, and she quit. She would spend the next ten years of her life taking various teaching jobs, but she rarely enjoyed them.

As busy as Anthony was, she still went out now and then with some young men. A few of them even proposed to her. Throughout her life, she would turn these men down. She remembered the powerful example of Mary Perkins and her career. She also recalled how her mother had lost everything she owned when her father lost his business. She was slowly becoming more aware of the way women were being treated. Later, she said she never married because "I never felt I could give up my life of freedom to become a man's housekeeper. When I was young, if a girl married poor, she became a housekeeper and a drudge," she added. "If she married wealthy, she became a pet and a doll."[6]

Anthony was also aware that a man's life as her husband would never be an easy one, due to her political passions. She wrote, "I would not consent that the man I loved . . . should unite his destinies in marriage with a political slave and pariah."[7] She was often saddened to hear that one of her friends had gotten married. She felt that her friend was losing focus on their cause for equality. As she said, "Independence is happiness."[8]

Refusing to marry, Anthony put her interests and passions elsewhere. She continued to teach. In 1845, her family moved to a thirty-two-acre farm in Rochester, New York, where they planted fruit orchards. Daniel began working in life insurance. He did well and the family grew stronger again. They also met other

Quakers. Some of them introduced the Anthonys to the work they were doing to help the nation's slaves. They met important supporters like Frederick Douglass and William Lloyd Garrison. Soon the family was going to antislavery meetings.

The following year, Susan became the head of the girls' department at Canajoharie Academy near Albany. She stayed with her cousin Margaret. Ignoring some of the rules of her Quaker lessons, she wore bright clothing and learned how to dance. She stayed for three years, then went back home again. Like many of the other Quakers of the time, she helped runaway slaves escape to the north through the Underground Railroad.

Anthony was becoming more and more interested in issues like slavery and temperance. She had been raised to believe that all people were equal. She also felt that using alcohol led to tragedy and unhappiness. Her family agreed with her. Two of her brothers even quit working on the farm so that they could become activists. In 1848, Daniel, Lucy, and their youngest child, Mary, attended the Woman's Rights Convention in Seneca Falls, New York. They listened closely to a passionate young speaker named Elizabeth Cady Stanton. She read her "Declaration of Rights and Sentiments" aloud. A new version of the Declaration of Independence, it listed twelve different ways to get equality for women. It included the areas of law, education, labor, morality, and religion. One of those ways was through the right to vote. When Stanton handed out copies, the Anthonys all signed it. It read:

> We hold these truths to be self-evident: that all men and women are created equal; that they are endowed by their Creator with certain inalienable rights; that among these are life, liberty and the pursuit of happiness . . .
>
> The history of mankind is a history of repeated injuries and usurpations on the part of man toward woman, having in direct object the establishment of an absolute tyrant over her . . .
>
> In view of this entire disfranchisement of one-half of the people of this country . . . because women do feel them-

Hundreds of women came to discuss their desire to be treated as equals at the 1848 Woman's Rights Convention in Seneca Falls, New York. Many men also attended, including Susan's father, Daniel Anthony.

selves aggrieved, . . . we insist that they have immediate admission to all rights and privileges which belong to them as citizens of the United States.[9]

The convention lasted for two days. Three hundred people came. In the end, eleven of the twelve ideas were passed unanimously. Only one passed by a very slim margin: the right for women to vote.

Anthony joined the Sons of Temperance, a group that focused on getting rid of alcohol. She became frustrated with them because they never talked about women's rights. She quit and formed the

The Sons of Temperance issued certificates declaring each "brother" a member. The group's motto was "Love, Purity and Fidelity." The group spread the word about the dangers of drinking alcohol.

Women's New York State Temperance Society. She was quickly elected president. She began making public speeches about the dangers of alcohol. Eventually, she quit teaching. Instead, her days were filled with organizing fairs and setting up fundraising dinners. She wrote, "Woman must take to her soul a purpose and then make circumstances conform to this purpose instead of forever singing the refrain 'if and if and if.' "[10] It came as little surprise when Anthony was elected to be the group's delegate to the state conventions.

Although she did not know it, Anthony's life had just taken a new direction. Soon she would meet the person who would help her define her purpose.

The World of Quakers

George Fox

George Fox (1625–1691) started the Quaker movement around the mid-seventeenth century in England. Originally they called themselves Friends of Truth. Later, that name was shortened to Friends. They were given the name Quakers because a judge jokingly stated that they "trembled at the word of the Lord." Today, they are known as the Religious Society of Friends.[11]

The center of the Quaker religion is the Inner Light. This light, they believe, is a part of God that is found deep within each and every person. They believe God speaks to their hearts. Many of their meetings are held in silence so that they can hear God's voice. This quietness is also one of the reasons they do not usually believe in music, dancing, and loud play. Many Quakers believe less in following the Bible than in constant prayer.

The Religious Society of Friends feels that each person has a personal relationship with God, so priests or ministers are not necessary. The Bible is a nice book to read, they suppose, but it was written by men under the power of the Holy Spirit. It does not contain the final words of God. Instead, a person just needs to listen to the Inner Voice in his or her heart.

Quakers have always believed that men and women are equal. They focus on simple living, including wearing plain clothes and using simple speech. They do not believe in any kind of violence. They are often involved in such actions as school and prison reform, helping those in need, improving employee conditions, and even providing ambulance services during wartime. Generally, they are a gentle people who believe in fairness, equality, and kindness for all people, regardless of race, gender, or beliefs.

Bloomers were a controversial invention. The short skirt and puffed pants allowed women to move more freely than their conventional layers of long skirts. However, many thought they were too revealing, and that they made women look more like men. They were viewed as another threat to traditional gender roles.

CHAPTER 3

Dedication and Determination

Anthony firmly believed in the ideals of her women's temperance group. She went so far as to state that drunkenness was grounds for divorce. This was a truly shocking idea for the times. As she worked to rid the world of alcohol, she also began to realize that the best way to do that was through giving women equal rights. It was the only way women would be heard with respect and have the power to end a marriage and keep custody of her children. Her focus began to shift. "Whoever controls work and wages, controls morals," she said.[1] "The fact is, women are in chains, and their servitude is all the more debasing because they do not realize it."[2]

Her feelings of frustration grew when she went to the state convention of the Sons of Temperance in 1851. When she rose to speak, she was clearly told, "The sisters were not invited here to speak, but to listen and learn."[3] Anthony stood up and left. So did several other women. Later that year, she went to a New York state teacher's meeting. Once again, she stood up to speak. The room went silent. No woman had ever tried to speak to this group before, even though many teachers were women. She could not begin until a vote was taken to see whether she should be allowed. She won, but just barely. Calmly, she explained that the

main reason teachers did not get the professional respect they wanted was because so many of them were female. Three men came up to her afterward and congratulated her for her courage in speaking up. However, most people—men and women—were shocked by her behavior.

Around this time, Anthony finally had the chance to meet the woman she had heard so much about: Elizabeth Cady Stanton. No other woman seemed as involved in getting rights for women as she was. Anthony was eager to talk to her. The first meeting between these two was rather disappointing. It only lasted for a few moments on a street corner. Knowing that they needed to spend time learning from each other, Stanton invited Anthony to come and stay at her home. The women knew right away that they had found a partner in the fight for suffrage.

For the next few years, Stanton and Anthony worked closely together to push the issue of women's rights into the awareness of the American people. They wrote and delivered countless speeches. Stanton wrote from her home, and Anthony traveled through more than fifty New York counties reading her powerful words. "I forged the thunderbolts, she fired them," described Stanton.[4] People were charged a quarter to get in to listen to Anthony speak. She used the money to pay for her food and shelter, but often it was not enough to cover those costs. She then had to use her own savings. It was a life she got used to, delivering up to 100 speeches a year for decades. She traveled by sleigh, coach, train, and on foot. She spoke out about women's rights, as well as antislavery issues. She put up posters, handed out flyers, and set up meetings. She had to adjust to little food, dirty lodgings, and being alone. She also had to cope with hostile people who threw things at her and called her every possible name. In some places, her image was hung in effigy. In others, it was dragged through the streets.

In 1860, because of Anthony's hard work, the Married Women's Property Act passed in New York. This new law allowed women to have rights over their own children, property, and wages, even if married. The action served as the model for other states to follow. In her diary, Anthony wrote, "There was no true freedom

for Woman without the possession of her property rights and . . . these rights could be obtained through legislation only. The sooner the demand was made of the legislation, the sooner would we be likely to obtain them."[5]

Another way that Stanton and Anthony affected society was a little more unusual. Like many other women, they found themselves frustrated and tired of the long, thick dresses and skirts they were forced to wear. They were difficult to move around in and were often quite hot. Stanton's friend Amelia Bloomer came up with another idea. She designed a skirt that was cut off just below the knees. A woman's legs were covered by loose, puffed-out pants that came to be known as bloomers. This would make walking and climbing stairs so much easier. Some women loved the invention. Stanton said, "To see my cousin, with a lamp in one hand and a baby in the other, walk upstairs with ease and grace, while, with flowing robes, I pulled myself up with difficulty, lamp and baby out of the question, readily convinced me that there was sore need of reform in women's dress."[6] It was not long before Stanton was wearing bloomers about. Anthony decided to give them a try as well. The bloomers did not work well for her. "The attention of my audience was fixed upon my clothes instead of my words," she wrote. "I learned the lesson then that to be successful a person must attempt but one reform . . . as the average mind can grasp but one idea at a time."[7] She went back to her long skirts.

In 1856, Anthony became the New York state agent for the American Anti-Slavery Association. She and Stanton kept working hard to keep the idea of women's rights in people's minds. Soon, they found their cause pushed completely away. A new and much bigger worry was facing the country: war. The issue of slavery, along with many other questions about states' rights, had finally become worth fighting over. In 1861, it all erupted as the Civil War. The women both realized that pushing for the right to vote would have to take a backseat to other issues. They also knew that fighting for African Americans to be free and considered as citizens with equal rights was related to their own cause. By bringing up the issue of rights for them, it brought up the issue

Isabella Baumfree was born into slavery in Ulster County, New York, in 1797. In 1826, she gained her freedom and took the name Sojourner Truth. She was a passionate speaker for equal rights for African Americans and for women.

of rights for all. As African American Sojourner Truth said, ". . . if colored men get their rights, and not colored women theirs . . . the colored men will be masters over the women and it will be just as bad as it was before."[8] After all, wrote Anthony, "The preamble of the Federal Constitution says, We, the people of the United States, not we, the white male citizens, not we, the male citizens; but we, the whole people, who formed this Union."[9]

With this hope in mind, the women threw their energy and support into helping get the Thirteenth Amendment (outlawing slavery) passed. In 1863, they formed the national Women's Loyal League to support antislavery events. Stanton was president. Anthony was secretary. They focused on getting signatures on a petition to support the new amendment. Within a year, they had gathered more than 400,000 names. As Anthony put it, "I don't want to die just as long as I can work. . . . I find that that the older

I get, the greater power I seem to have to help the world; I am like a snowball—the further I am rolled the more I gain."[10]

When the war ended in 1865, slavery was outlawed. The Thirteenth Amendment was approved. The nation turned its eyes to the proposed Fourteenth Amendment next. It stated that all people (including African Americans) were citizens with equal rights. This included the right to vote. However, this amendment included the word "male" for the first time. It pointedly left out women from these same rights.

Anthony and Stanton formed the American Equal Rights Association to fight for the rights of both women and African Americans. Anthony was shocked and disappointed to find that all those she had helped during the war were now abandoning her and her cause for women. They were not fighting at her side for what she felt women deserved, as she had expected.

It was not long before a growing hostility developed between those for women's rights and those for African American rights. Frederick Douglass, a longtime supporter of Anthony's cause, decided that he had to dedicate his time and efforts to getting the Fourteenth Amendment passed as it was. It took months for this amendment for racial equality to be ratified, and by the time it finally did in June, Anthony and Stanton had already formed the National Woman Suffrage Association (NWSA). In January 1868, they also began publishing a newspaper called *The Revolution.* Its motto was "Men their rights and nothing more; women their rights and nothing less."[11]

Anthony continued to travel to further her cause. She spread the word about suffrage wherever she could. At one point, she found a traveling companion in George Francis Train. He was a millionaire. He was also a racist. For two years, he traveled with Anthony, writing about the experience and speaking to crowds. He also funded *The Revolution.* By 1870, the newspaper had over 3,000 readers. Then, Train's interest began to fade. As he went in other directions, so did his money. Anthony could not afford to keep publishing. When she finally sold the paper for $1, she had a $10,000 debt to pay. It would take a long time, but she eventually paid it all off through her fees for speaking.

Although Frederick Douglass was a strong supporter of Anthony's, in the end he focused on getting rights for African Americans. The Fourteenth Amendment passed in 1867 and was ratified in 1868.

The war had slowed down the cause for women by years. Now, in 1868, it had a further setback as many supporters split from the movement to support the African Americans and the Fourteenth Amendment. Anthony, however, was not defeated. Despite the obstacles, she continued to feel, as she said: "Failure is impossible!" She was about to put that statement to a test that would shock the entire nation.

Elizabeth Cady Stanton

Elizabeth Cady Stanton was as different from Anthony as anyone could imagine. Where Anthony was single, Stanton was married and mother to seven children. Anthony was the speaker. Stanton was the writer. Anthony was the planner, keeping track of every detail in her speeches. Stanton was the emotional dynamo behind her words. Anthony was stark and serious-looking. Stanton was usually smiling. Together they made one of history's most effective teams.

In the first volume of Stanton and Anthony's *History of Woman Suffrage*, Stanton explained their relationship this way:

> In writing we did better work together than either could do alone. While she is slow and analytical in composition, I am rapid and synthetic. I am the better writer; she the better critic. She supplied the facts and statistics, I the philosophy and rhetoric, and together we made arguments which have stood unshaken by the storms of thirty long years; arguments that no man has answered.[12]

Elizabeth Cady was born in Johnstown, New York, in 1815. Her father was a judge and state legislator who believed in educating his daughters. Elizabeth attended the Troy Female Seminary. She developed interests in everything from riding horses to learning Latin. Soon after, she became involved with the abolitionist movement.

In 1840, Elizabeth met Henry Stanton. He was also an activist. Soon, the two were married. Their honeymoon was taken at the World Anti-Slavery Convention. There, the women were kept in an area behind a curtain so that they could be neither seen nor heard. This did not please Stanton at all. She resolved to do something about it. It was she that the Anthonys heard in 1848 when they went to the Woman's Rights Convention. She had organized the event with her friend Lucretia Mott.

The friendship between Stanton (left) and Anthony (right) would last for decades. When Stanton died in 1902, Anthony was devastated. She wrote that she was "too crushed to speak. If I had died first she would have found beautiful phrases to describe our friendship, but I cannot put it into words."[13] In a letter she wrote, "It seems impossible—that the voice is hushed—that I have longed to hear for 50 years—longed to get her opinion of things—before I knew exactly where I stood—It is all at sea."[14]

Judge Ward Hunt was appointed U.S. Supreme Court Justice in 1872. While presiding over the famous Anthony trial, he gave Anthony the chance to speak only after her sentence was pronounced. Even then, he tried to stop her before she had finished.

CHAPTER
4

Into the Courtroom

For almost a quarter century, Susan B. Anthony had fought to gain women the right to vote. She believed that they wanted, needed, and deserved it. Finally she grew tired of waiting for the rest of the world to agree with her. On November 5, 1872, with the support of three of her sisters, she marched down to the local barber shop and demanded that voting inspectors Beverly Jones, William Hall, and Edwin Marsh allow her to register. They refused, of course, but that didn't stop her. She pulled out copies of the Fourteenth Amendment and began reading it to the shocked men. When reading the law did not seem to make any difference, she started threatening them. "If you still refuse us our rights as citizens," she shouted, "I will bring charges against you in Criminal Court and I will sue each of you personally for large, exemplary damages! I know I can win!"[1] The men did not know what to do. They debated the topic for an hour. Finally, they allowed the women to register. Moments later, Anthony and fourteen other women voted for the very first time.

Her excitement over her chance to vote is clearly seen in a letter she wrote to Stanton that same day. "Well I have been & gone & done it!!—positively voted the Republican ticket—strait this A.M. at 7 Oclock—& swore my vote in at that—was registered on

Friday & 15 [sic] other women followed suit in this ward—then on Sunday others some 20 or thirty other women tried to register, but all save two were refused—all my three sisters voted . . . I hope the morning's telegrams will tell of many women all over the country trying to vote . . . what strides we might make this winter—But I'm awful tired—for five days I have been on the constant run—but to splendid purpose—So all right—I hope you voted too."[2]

Their victory was short-lived. Two weeks later, on November 18, Anthony was arrested. So were the voting inspectors who allowed her and the other women to vote. Anthony was upset that these men had been arrested. She felt they had done nothing wrong. Even though they were charged, she asked some of her political friends to see that they were released. Five days later, they were. The trial hearing was set for December 23. Each woman was released on bail, but Anthony refused to pay it. Angered by her attitude, Judge Ward Hunt doubled her fine to $1,000. She refused to pay the fine. She knew that if she did not pay, she could take her case to the Supreme Court of Appeals. Against her wishes, her lawyer, Henry Selden, who could not stand to see her behind bars, paid the fine for her.

Anthony knew just what to do while waiting for her trial to begin. She traveled to fifty towns throughout New England, educating the people about women's rights through a speech called "Is It a Crime for a Citizen of the United States to Vote?" In it, she said, "Friends and Fellow Citizens; I stand before you to-night, under indictment for the alleged crime of having voted at the last Presidential election, without having a lawful right to vote. It shall be my work this evening to prove to you that in thus voting, I not only committed no crime, but, instead, simply exercised my citizen's right, guaranteed to me and all United States citizens by the National Constitution, beyond the power of any State to deny."[3] She talked to so many people that prosecuting attorney Crowley declared the trial had to be moved to another county in order to have an impartial jury.

At last, on January 24, 1873, Anthony's trial began. Lawyer Henry Selden opened her defense by saying, "This is a case of no

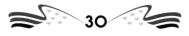

Many cartoons, such as this one from New York's Daily Graphic, depicted Anthony as a masculine woman out to control the world. Note the other gender role reversals in the cartoon: a female police officer, a man holding a baby, and a man carrying a basket of food.

ordinary magnitude, although many might regard it as one of very little importance."[4] He spoke for three hours. The question before the court was not whether she had voted but whether her voting was a crime. Plus, if Anthony truly believed she had the right to vote, could she be found guilty of unlawful voting? Selden said, "If the same act had been done by her brother . . . the act would have been . . . honorable . . . but having been done by a woman, it is said to be a crime."[5]

Anthony was not allowed to speak on her own behalf. Judge Hunt determined that she was not competent as a witness since she was a female. His opinion regarding her guilt was clear from the beginning. In her diary, Anthony wrote that the trial was "the greatest judicial outrage history has ever recorded! We were convicted before we had a hearing and the trial was a mere farce."[6]

When it came time for sentencing, the jury was not allowed to speak. Instead, Judge Hunt pulled a piece of paper out of his pocket and began to read it. "The Fourteenth Amendment gives

no right to a woman to vote and the voting by Miss Anthony was in violation of the law," he said. "Upon this evidence I suppose there is no question for the jury and that the jury should be directed to find a verdict of guilty."[7]

Selden was outraged that no one had been allowed to speak on Anthony's behalf and that the jury was silenced. He demanded a new trial but was denied. "No juror spoke a word during the trial, from the time they were impaneled to the time they were discharged," he wrote.[8] On January 24, Anthony was found guilty of "knowingly, wrongfully and unlawfully voting without having a lawful right to vote . . . the said Susan B. Anthony being then and there a person of the female sex."[9]

After she was found guilty, the judge asked, "Has the prisoner anything to say why sentence should not be pronounced?"[10] The people in the courtroom were stunned when Anthony stood up. Finally given the chance to speak her mind, she filled the place with passionate words. Judge Hunt tried to stop her six times—but failed each time. In part, Anthony said:

> Yes, your honor, I have many things to say; for in your ordered verdict of guilty, you have trampled under foot every vital principle of our government. My natural rights, my civil rights, my political rights, my judicial rights, are all alike ignored. . . .
>
> When I was brought before your honor for trial, I hoped for a broad and liberal interpretation of the Constitution and its recent amendments, that should declare . . . equality of rights the national guarantee to all persons born or naturalized in the United States. But failing to get this justice—failing, even, to get a trial by a jury not of my peers—I ask not leniency at your hands—but rather the full rigors of the law. . . . May it please your honor, I shall never pay a dollar of your unjust penalty. . . . And I shall earnestly and persistently continue to urge all women to the practical recognition of the old revolutionary maxim, that "Resistance to tyranny is obedience to God."[11]

Anthony hangs a banner to remind her followers that no matter what, "Failure is impossible!" Even when she lost her case in front of Judge Hunt, many declared the trial a victory for Anthony. It helped spread her message about women's rights.

Judge Hunt fined Anthony $100. As promised, she refused to pay it. She never did either.

Even though Anthony lost her trial, the event helped spread the word about the ongoing suffrage efforts to the rest of the world. Newspapers wrote editorials. Reporters covered daily trial happenings. One reporter wrote, "The woman suffragists love her for her good works, the audience for her brightness and wit, and the multitude of press representatives for her frank, plain, open, business-like way."[12]

Anthony was a hero to many. Feeling sorry for her made them more open to the possibility of women's rights. Just to make sure

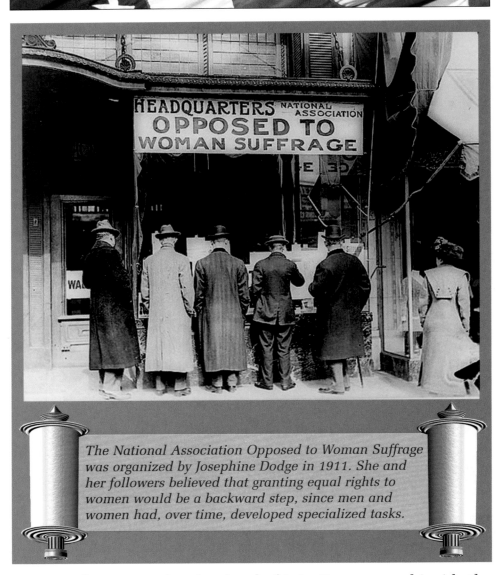

The National Association Opposed to Woman Suffrage was organized by Josephine Dodge in 1911. She and her followers believed that granting equal rights to women would be a backward step, since men and women had, over time, developed specialized tasks.

everyone knew exactly what level of injustice occurred inside the courtroom, Anthony printed 3,000 copies of the trial's transcripts. She gave them to libraries, politicians, and teachers. As one New York newspaper wrote, "If it is a mere question of who got the best of it, Miss Anthony is still ahead. She has voted and the American Constitution has survived the shock. Fining her one hundred dollars does not rule out the fact that women voted and went home, and the world jogged on as before."[13]

The Susan B. Anthony House

Sitting on Madison Street in Rochester, New York, is Susan B. Anthony's home (left). She lived there from 1866 until her death forty years later. Although she spent most of her time traveling to gain support for women's rights, when she did come home to rest, it was there. Her home is where she was arrested, where she worked with Stanton, and where she worked on the multivolume *History of Woman Suffrage.*

Built before the Civil War, the house is now a visitor's center that people can tour to get a glimpse of Anthony's life. Inside, they can see photographs of Stanton and Anthony, some of Anthony's clothes, and other artifacts. Mary, Susan Anthony's youngest sister, also lived in the house, and her bedroom is there. Like her older sister, Mary was rather outspoken. She became the first woman principal in Rochester. She had refused to take the job, however, until the school system promised to pay her the same amount of money as the man who had had the job before her. When she paid her 1901 tax bill, she also took the time to write on it, "Enclosed find $62.63 city tax which I pay under protest, still believing that taxation without representation is as great a tyranny today . . . as it was in 1776. . . . Yours for Equal Rights . . ."[14]

Some of the other pieces that visitors can spot in the Anthony house include the small alligator bag that Susan carried with her on all her travels, her eyeglasses, copies of *The Revolution,* and a marble bust of Susan B. Anthony. It is on loan from the Metropolitan Museum of Art.

The Anthony house has been improved twice since 1998. In 2006, the organization was planning to restore the inside. The carpets, floors, trim, lighting, stairs, paint, and wallpaper were all to be updated. An online virtual tour of the house is available at http://www.susanbanthonyhouse.org/.

Although Stanton and Anthony were opposites in so many ways, they made one of the most impressive teams in history. Together they helped to write the multivolume History of Woman Suffrage, *which they filled with quotes by some of the most important women in the women's movement.*

CHAPTER
5

Waiting and Hoping Until the End

The trial might have been over but the fight certainly was not. Anthony did not let her defeat in the courtroom slow down her mission at all. She continued to pursue equal rights for women for the rest of her life.

In 1880, she began appearing before the U.S. Senate Judiciary Committee. Not long after, she and Stanton published the first of three volumes of their *History of Woman Suffrage*. At the age of sixty-three, Anthony made her first trip to Europe. She established the International Council of Women while there. More than fifty different organizations from Europe, Canada, and the United States sent representatives to be part of the new council.

Next, Anthony and Stanton formed the National American Women Suffrage Association (NAWSA). Stanton was the first president. When she retired in 1892, Anthony took over the role. She kept it for eight years, not retiring until the age of eighty. During her years there, she worked on promoting a state-by-state campaign for women's rights. If an individual state decided it was all right for women to vote, it could be permitted. The first place to do so was the Wyoming Territory; however it was not a state yet. One night in 1890, while Anthony was on stage giving yet another speech, she was handed a telegram announcing that Wyoming had been admitted as a state. At last, one state on the map legally allowed women to vote. It was soon followed by Colorado, Idaho, and Utah.

In the early 1890s, the team of Stanton and Anthony finally began to drift in two different directions. Stanton had become rather critical of Christianity. She felt that organized religion often forced women to remain the weaker sex in a marriage. This attitude distanced her from many other suffragettes, including Anthony. Although their paths began to diverge, the two remained friends for the rest of their lives.

As the nineteenth century gave way to the twentieth, the fight for women's rights continued. At age seventy-five Anthony collapsed from exhaustion on stage in Lakeside, Ohio, but she kept traveling and speaking for six more years. When the University of Rochester said that they would admit female students if they could raise the $100,000 they needed to expand their campus, it was Anthony who came up with the last $8,000, minutes before the midnight deadline. She had gone door to door calling on her friends and supporters in order to raise the money.

In 1902, Anthony lost her dear friend and partner, Elizabeth Cady Stanton. It was an emotional blow from which she never quite recovered.

In 1904, Anthony's hard work was honored by a White House reception held by President Theodore Roosevelt. Her very last public appearance was in 1906 at her eighty-sixth birthday celebration at the NAWSA convention. She recognized that while great strides has been made during her lifetime, the vote women needed, wanted, and deserved was still not theirs. It would belong to the next generation of determined and dedicated women to make it happen. "We little dreamed when we began this contest that half a century later we would be compelled to leave the finish of the battle to another generation of women," she said. "But our hearts are filled with joy to know that they enter this task equipped with a college education, with business experience, with the freely admitted right to speak in public—all of which were denied to women fifty years ago."[1]

A few weeks later, on March 13, Anthony died of pneumonia at her Madison Street home. Her funeral was held at the Central Presbyterian Church. Despite the huge snowstorm that blanketed the city, more than 10,000 people came to the ceremony to pay their respects to this strong and powerful woman. Carrie Chapman Catt, the new head of NAWSA, said, "Her 86 years measure a movement whose results have been more far-reaching in the change of conditions, social, civil and political, than those of any war of revolution since history began."[2] In her eulogy, Reverend Anna Howard Shaw said:

> Your flags at half-mast tell of a nation's loss, but there are no symbols and no words which can tell the love and sorrow which fill our hearts. And yet out of the depths of our grief arise feelings of truest gratitude for the beauty, the tenderness, the nobility of example, of our peerless leader's life. There is no such death for such as she. There are no last words of love. The ages to come will revere her name. Unnumbered generations of the children of men shall rise up to call her blessed. Her words, her work, and her character will go on to brighten the pathway and bless the lives of all peoples. That which seems death to our unseeing eyes is to her translation. Her work will not be finished, nor will her last word be spoken while there remains a wrong to be righted, or a fettered life to be freed in all the earth.[3]

It would be another fourteen years before Anthony's dream for women came true. Her fight was continued by other determined women, including Harriot Stanton Blatch and Nora Blatch (Stanton's daughter and granddaughter). In 1913, more than 5,000 suffragists from all over the country gathered in Washington, D.C. They marched in protest the day before President Woodrow Wilson's inauguration. Four years later, they staged protests outside the White House. As the nation fought World War I, they wanted the vote more than ever. They carried banners that read, "Mr. President, how long must women wait for liberty."[4] Many were arrested and put in prison. They suffered from brutal and

On December 6, 1915, thousands of women marched at the U.S. capital to demonstrate for their right vote. A federal woman suffrage amendment was introduced in the House of Representatives that day and in the Senate the next.

uncaring treatment there. As soon as they were released, however, they returned to the sidewalks to protest once again—and again they would be arrested. On November 14, 1917, a workhouse superintendent and his guards lost patience with these women and attacked them. The inmates were beaten, choked, and stabbed, then thrown into concrete cells. Two weeks later, a judge released the women. The event became known as the Night of Terror.

Although it would take three more years to win the right to vote, these women had shown the world their strength and their

Suffragist Anna Howard Shaw held degrees in theology and medicine. She carried on Anthony's work as president of NAWSA (1904–1915), delivering powerful speeches for the movement. She died on July 2, 1919, one month after the Nineteenth Amendment was passed to the states for ratification.

willingness to fight for what they deserved. Anthony would have been proud. She probably would have told them, as she once told Anna Howard Shaw, "No matter what is done or is not done, how you are criticized or misunderstood, or what efforts are made to block your path, remember that the only fear you need have is the fear of not standing by the thing you believe is right."[5]

When the Nineteenth Amendment giving every woman in the country the right to vote was finally passed in 1920, it came as little surprise that it was nicknamed the Susan B. Anthony Amendment. It was her courage, conviction, and resolve that led to something the country now considers completely normal: the right of all its citizens to vote.

The Night of Terror

Without the determination of other women suffragists, such as Alice Paul (left), Susan B. Anthony's work may never have been completed. Paul had multiple degrees, including several PhDs. She worked hard to secure women's rights in the United Kingdom and in doing so was imprisoned three times. Each time, she went on a hunger strike to pressure the government.

When Paul returned to the United States, she became the chairman of the National American Women Suffrage Association. During the presidential campaign of 1916, Paul and other suffragists campaigned against Woodrow Wilson because of his lack of support for the suffrage amendment. Many of them took signs and banners and began picketing the White House. Known as the Silent Sentinels, they were the first group in U.S. history to stage a nonviolent civil disobedience campaign.

Although the women were warned to stop, they kept on, and soon the arrests began. What happened next, however, became a dark spot in human rights history. In their cells, the women were given worm-infested food, polluted water, and vicious beatings. Some of the women, including Paul, began a hunger strike once again. This time, Paul was tied to a chair and force-fed until she vomited. In an excerpt from an article about the event written by feminist Sonia Pressman Fuentes, Paul revealed:

> . . . as many as forty guards with clubs went on a rampage, brutalizing thirty-three jailed suffragists. They beat Lucy Burns, chained her hands to the cell bars above her head, and left her there for the night. They hurled Dora Lewis into a dark cell, smashed her head against an iron bed and knocked her out cold. Her cellmate, Alice Cosu, who believed Mrs. Lewis to be dead, suffered a heart attack. According to other affidavits, other women were grabbed, dragged, beaten, choked, slammed, pinched, twisted, and kicked.[6]

When Paul refused to end her hunger strike, she was taken to the prison hospital. No one was allowed to see her. When she still refused to eat, she was taken by stretcher to the psychiatric ward and considered a mental patient. After a week, she was at last released by lawyer Dudley Field Malone. She continued the fight for the rest of her life.

Chapter Notes

Chapter 1   A Knock on the Door

1. Doug Linder, *The Trial of Susan B. Anthony for Illegal Voting, 2001,* http://www.law.umkc.edu/faculty/projects/ftrials/anthony/sbaaccount.html.

2. Architect of the Capitol, "Relocation of Portrait Monument to Lucretia Mott, Elizabeth Cady Stanton, and Susan B. Anthony" http://www.aoc.gov/cc/art/rotunda/suffrage_move.cfm.

Chapter 2   Growing Up, Taking Stands

1. Susan B. Anthony, http://www.history.rochester.edu/class/suffrage/Anthony.html.

2. Kathleen Barry, *Susan B. Anthony: A Biography of a Singular Feminist* (New York: New York University Press, 1988), p. 18.

3. Diana Star Helmer, *Women Suffragists* (New York: Facts on File, 1998), p. 16.

4. Geoffrey C. Ward and Ken Burns, *Not for Ourselves Alone* (New York: Alfred A. Knopf, 1999), p. 27.

5. Ida Husted Harper, *Life and Work of Susan B. Anthony* (New York: Arno Publishing and New York Times, 1969), p. 35.

6. Doug Linder, Susan B. Anthony: A Biography, 2001. http://www.law.umkc.edu/faculty/projects/ftrials/anthony/sbabiog.html

7. Helmer, p. 21.

8. Global Renaissance Alliance, http://www.renaissancealliance.org/silenc/quotes.htm.

9. Jerome Agel, *Words That Make America Great* (New York: Random House, 1997), pp. 112–114.

10. Helmer, p. 17.

11. Hans Weening, *Meeting the Spirit—An Introduction to Quaker Beliefs and Practices* http://emes.quaker.eu.org/documents/files/meeting-the-spirit.html

Chapter 3   Dedication and Determination

1. Diana Star Helmer, *Women Suffragists* (New York: Facts on File, 1998), p. 18.

2. Jennifer Thaney, "Re-Imagining Feminism," WomenPress.com, November 8, 2000, http://www.rebeccawalker.com/article_2000_re-imagining-feminism.htm

3. Helmer, p. 18.

4. Elisabeth Griffin, *Elizabeth Cady Stanton: In Her Own Right* (New York: Oxford University Press, 1984), p. 74.

5. Helmer, p. 19.

6. Elizabeth Cady Stanton, *Eighty Years and More* (New York: Schocken Books, 1971), p. 201.

7. Ida Husted Harper, *Life and Work of Susan B. Anthony* (New York: Arno Publishing and New York Times, 1969), p. 115.

8. Helmer, p. 24.

9. Sue Heinemann, *Amazing Women in American History* (New York: Stonesong Press, 1998), p. 46.

10. Susan B Anthony quotes, womenshistory.about.com/cs/quotes/a/qu_s_b_anthony.htm

11. Barbara Holland, *They Went Whistling: Women Wayfarers, Warriors, Runaways and Renegades* (New York: Pantheon Books, 2001), p. 242.

12. Deborah G. Felder, *The 100 Most Influential Women of All Time* (New York: Citadel Press, 2001), p. 26.

13. Kathleen Barry, *Susan B. Anthony: A Biography of a Singular Feminist* (New York: New York University Press, 1988), p. 340.

14. Rutgers University, Papers of Elizabeth Cady Stanton and Susan B. Anthony, "Susan B. Anthony to Ida Husted Harper upon the death of Elizabeth Cady Stanton, 28 October 1902," http://ecssba.rutgers.edu/docs/sbatoharp.html.

Chapter 4   Into the Courtroom

1. Doug Linder, *The Trial of Susan B. Anthony for Illegal Voting, 2001,* http://www.law.umkc.edu/faculty/projects/ftrials/anthony/sbaaccount.html

2. SBA letter to Anthony's close friend, Elizabeth Cady Stanton, November 5, 1872 http://www.law.umkc.edu/faculty/projects/ftrials/Anthony/voteletters.html

3. Susan B. Anthony Trial Page: Address of Susan B. Anthony, "Is it a Crime for a Citizen of the United States to Vote?" http://www.law.umkc.edu/faculty/projects/ftrials/anthony/anthonyaddress.html

4. Susan B. Anthony Trial Page: Opening Statement for the Defense in the Case of *United States vs Susan B. Anthony,* http://www.law.umkc.edu/faculty/projects/ftrials/anthony/defeopen.html

5. Ida Husted Harper, *Life and Work of Susan B. Anthony* (New York: Arno Publishing and New York Times, 1969), p. 437.

6. Linder.

7. Ibid.

8. Ibid.

9. Ibid.

10. Ibid.

11. Ibid.

12. Lynn Sherr, *Failure Is Impossible: Susan B. Anthony in Her Own Words* (New York: Three Rivers Press, 1996), p. 81.

13. Linder.

14. The Susan B. Anthony House Organization, Tour, Second Floor, http://www.susanbanthonyhouse.org/tour2.html

Chapter 5   Waiting and Hoping Until the End

1. Deborah G. Felder, *The 100 Most Influential Women of All Time* (New York: Citadel Press, 2001), p. 29.

2. Ida Husted Harper, *Life and Work of Susan B. Anthony* (New York: Arno Publishing and New York Times, 1969), p. 438.

3. Rutgers University, Papers of Elizabeth Cady Stanton and Susan B. Anthony, "Eulogy Delivered by the Reverend Anna Howard Shaw at Susan B. Anthony's Funeral; Rochester, New York, 15 March 1906," http://ecssba.rutgers.edu/docs/shaw.html

4. William and Mary Lavender, "Suffragists Storm Over Washington D.C. in 1917," *American History*, October 2003, http://www.historynet.com/culture/womens_history/3028551.html

5. Ann Bausum, *With Courage and Cloth: Winning the Fight for a Woman's Right to Vote* (Washington, D.C.: National Geographic, 2004), p. 92.

6. Sonia Pressman Fuentes, "Three United States Feminists—A Personal Tribute," *Jewish Affairs*, 53.1 (Johannesburg, South Africa, 1998): 37; available online at http://www.moondance.org/1998/winter98/nonfiction/alice.html

Chronology

1820	Susan B. Anthony is born on February 15 in Adams, Massachusetts
1835	Attends Deborah Moulson's Female Seminary
1837	Returns home to help family after economic depression
1839	Begins teaching at boarding school in New Rochelle, New York
1845	Anthony family moves to farm in Rochester, New York
1846	Begins teaching at the Canajoharie Academy in Albany
1848	Family attends the Woman's Rights Convention in Seneca Falls, New York
1851	Susan meets Elizabeth Cady Stanton
1856	Becomes New York state agent for the American Anti-Slavery Association
1860	Helps to get the Married Women's Property Act passed in New York
1863	Forms the National Women's Loyal League
1868	Begins publishing *The Revolution*
1872	Is arrested after voting in November 5 election
1873	Is tried and found guilty of unlawful voting on January 24
1880	Appears before the U.S. Senate Judiciary Committee
1883	Takes first trip to Europe; establishes the International Council of Women
1892	Becomes president of the National American Women Suffrage Association
1902	Is devastated when Elizabeth Cady Stanton dies
1904	Is honored at the White House by President Theodore Roosevelt
1906	Dies of pneumonia at the age of eighty-six

Timeline in History

1776	Abigail Adams writes to her husband, delegate John Adams, at the Continental Congress to "remember the ladies" as he works on the Declaration of Independence.
1790	The colony of New Jersey grants the vote to "all free inhabitants."
1807	Women's right to vote is repealed.
1830s	Female antislavery associations begin to form.
1840	The World Anti-Slavery Convention is held in London.
1848	First Woman's Rights Convention is held in Seneca Falls, New York.
1850	First National Woman's Rights Convention is held in Worchester, Massachusetts.
1861	The Civil War begins.
1865	The Civil War ends.
1868	The Fourteenth Amendment, which grants citizenship to anyone born or naturalized in the U.S., and provides equal protection to them all, is ratified.
1870	The Fifteenth Amendment, granting African American men the right to vote, passes.
1871	Anti-Suffrage Society is formed.
1874	Women's Christian Temperance Union is formed.
1878	Women's suffrage amendment is first introduced in U.S. Congress.
1890	Wyoming grants women's suffrage.
1895	Elizabeth Cady Stanton publishes *The Woman's Bible*.
1896	Idaho grants women's suffrage.
1907	Harriot Stanton Blatch, Elizabeth Stanton's daughter, forms the Equality League of Self-Supporting Women.
1910	Washington state grants women's suffrage.
1911	California grants women's suffrage.
1913	Suffragettes picket President Woodrow Wilson's inauguration.
1915	A federal woman suffrage amendment is introduced in Congress.
1917	Women protesters are beaten in their jail cells during the Night of Terror in Washington, D.C.
1920	The Nineteenth Amendment passes, granting U.S. women the right to vote.
1961	President John F. Kennedy sets up the President's Commission on the Status of Women.
1963	Congress passes the Equal Pay Act, granting women equal pay for equal work.
1966	The National Organization for Women (NOW) is founded by Betty Friedan.
1972	The Equal Rights Amendment is passed by Congress.
1974	The Equal Credit Opportunity Act is passed.
1984	Geraldine Ferraro becomes the first female vice-presidential candidate.
2006	With the November elections, Nancy Pelosi is set to become the first female Speaker of the House, the third highest political office in the U.S.

Further Reading

For Young Adults

Kendall, Martha E. *Susan B. Anthony: Voice for Women's Voting Rights*. Berkeley Heights, New Jersey: Enslow Publishers, 1997.

Monroe, Judy. *Susan B. Anthony Women's Voting Rights Trial*. Berkeley Heights, New Jersey: Enslow Publishers, 2002.

Monsell, Helen Albee. *Susan B. Anthony: Champion of Women's Rights*. London: Aladdin Books, 1986.

Nash, Carol Rust. *The Fight for Women's Right to Vote in American History*. Berkeley Heights, New Jersey: Enslow Publishers, 1998.

Sherr, Lynn. Failure *Is Impossible: Susan B. Anthony in Her Own Words* (New York: Three Rivers Press,1996).

Ward, Geoffrey C. *Not for Ourselves Alone: The Story of Elizabeth Cady Stanton and Susan B. Anthony* (New York: Knopf Books, 2001).

Weidt, Maryann. *Fighting for Equal Rights: A Story about Susan B. Anthony* (Minneapolis: Carolrhoda Books, 2003).

Works Consulted

Bausum, Ann. *With Courage and Cloth: Winning the Fight for a Woman's Right to Vote*. Washington, D.C.: National Geographic, 2004.

Bohannen, Lisa F. *Failure Is Impossible: The Story of Susan B. Anthony*. Greensboro, North Carolina: Morgan Reynolds Publishing, 2001.

Buhle, Mari Jo, and Paul Buhle, editors. *The Concise History of Woman Suffrage*. Chicago: University of Illinois Press, 2005.

Felder, Deborah G. *The 100 Most Influential Women of All Time*. New York: Citadel Press, 2001.

Heinemann, Sue. *Amazing Women in American History*. New York: Stonesong Press, 1998.

Helmer, Diana Star. *Women Suffragists*. New York: Facts on File, 1998.

Holland, Barbara. *They Went Whistling: Women Wayfarers, Warriors, Runaways and Renegades*. New York: Pantheon Books, 2001.

Leone, Bruno, executive editor. *The Women's Rights Movement*. San Diego: Greenhaven Press, 1996.

Sherr, Lynn. *Failure Is Impossible: Susan B. Anthony in Her Own Words*. New York: Three Rivers Press, 1996.

Stanton, Elizabeth Cady. *The Selected Papers of Elizabeth Cady Stanton and Susan B. Anthony: Against an Aristocracy of Sex, 1866–1873*. Piscataway, New Jersey: Rutgers University Press, 2000.

On the Internet

Architect of the Capitol, "Relocation of Portrait Monument to Lucretia Mott, Elizabeth Cady Stanton, and Susan B. Anthony,"
http://www.aoc.gov/cc/art/rotunda/suffrage_move.cfm

The Equal Rights Amendment
www.equalrightsamendment.org

Famous American Trials: The Trial of Susan B. Anthony, 1873
www.law.umkc.edu/faculty/projects/ftrials/anthony/sbahome.html

Friends World Committee for Consultation
http://fwccworld.org/

Susan B Anthony
www.history.rochester.edu/class/sba/first.htm

Susan B. Anthony House
www.susanbanthonyhouse.org

The Religious Society of Friends
www.quaker.org

Rochester History Resources
www.history.rochester.edu

Rutgers University, Papers of Elizabeth Cady Stanton and Susan B. Anthony
http://ecssba.rutgers.edu

Glossary

abolitionist (aa-buh-LIH-shuh-nist)
A person who fought to end slavery.

aggrieved (uh-GREEVD)
Suffering because rights have been denied.

creditors (KREH-dih-turs)
People who lend money.

disfranchisement (dis-FRAN-chyz-munt)
Being denied of a basic right, especially the right to vote.

drudge (DRUJ)
One who works hard at boring tasks.

effigy (EH-feh-jee)
A crude figure or dummy representing a hated person or group.

eulogy (YOO-lih-jee)
A praiseful speech given at a funeral.

exemplary (eg-ZEMPT-luh-ree)
Serving as an example; worthy of imitation.

farce (FARS)
A ridiculous or meaningless show; a mockery.

impartial (im-PAR-shul)
Not biased or showing favoritism.

inauguration (in-aw-gyuh-RAY-shun)
The ceremony marking the beginning of a person's time in political office.

pariah (puh-RYE-ah)
An outcast.

ratified (RAA-tih-fyd)
Gave formal approval of, usually by signing.

seminary (SEH-mih-nay-ree)
A school for religious training.

suffragist (SUH-frih-jist)
A person who works for voting rights, especially for women.

temperance (TEM-prins)
Moderation in behavior, especially regarding use of alcohol.

tyranny (TEE-ruh-nee)
A government with a single ruler, who rules with absolute power.

unanimously (yoo-NAA-nuh-mus-lee)
Being in complete agreement, having the same opinions or votes.

usurpation (yoo-sur-PAY-shun)
The taking of a right or possession by force.

Index